PRE TEEN PRESSURES

DIVORCE

by Debra Goldentyer

RSVP
RAINTREE
STECK-VAUGHN
PUBLISHERS
The Steck-Vaughn Company

Austin, Texas

Consultants

Antonia Flint, Psychotherapist, Trinity Counseling Service, Princeton, NJ

William B. Presnell, Clinical Member, American Association for Marriage and Family Therapy

Developed for Steck-Vaughn Company by
Visual Education Corporation, Princeton, New Jersey
Project Director: Jewel Moulthrop
Editor: Paula McGuire
Editorial Assistant: Jacqueline Morais
Photo Research: Sara Matthews
Electronic Preparation: Cynthia C. Feldner, Manager; Fiona Torphy
Production Supervisor: Ellen Foos
Electronic Production: Lisa Evans-Skopas, Manager; Elise Dodeles, Deirdre Sheean, Isabelle Verret
Interior Design: Maxson Crandall

Raintree Steck-Vaughn Publishers staff
Editor: Kathy DeVico
Project Manager: Joyce Spicer

Photo Credits: Cover: © David Young-Wolff/PhotoEdit; 6: © David Young-Wolff/PhotoEdit; 8: © Michael Newman/PhotoEdit; 10: © Batt Johnson/Unicorn Stock Photos; 13: © David Young-Wolff/PhotoEdit; 17: © Robert Brenner/PhotoEdit; 19: © Kathy Ferguson/ PhotoEdit; 20: © Robert W. Ginn/Unicorn Stock Photos; 24: © Royce Bair/Unicorn Stock Photos; 27: © Jonathan Nourok/PhotoEdit; 29: © Tom McCarthy/Unicorn Stock Photos; 39: © David Young-Wolff/PhotoEdit; 42: © Aneal Vohra/Unicorn Stock Photos

Library of Congress Cataloging-in-Publication Data
Goldentyer, Debra, 1960–
    Divorce/by Debra Goldentyer.
        p.   cm. — (Preteen pressures)
    Includes bibliographical references and index.
    Summary: Describes divorce and explains how to deal with the breaking up of your parents' marriage.
    ISBN 0-8172-5030-1
    1. Divorce—United States—Juvenile literature.   [1. Divorce.]   I. Title. II. Series.
HQ834.G66 1998
306.89—dc21   97-17930
                                              CIP
                                            AC

Printed and bound in the United States
1 2 3 4 5 6 7 8 9 0 LB 01 00 99 98 97

CONTENTS

INTRODUCTION

Are your parents going through a divorce? Are a friend's parents divorcing? Divorce is upsetting for everyone involved. And if it's your own parents who are divorcing, you are very much involved. Divorce causes many changes. You are used to living with your mother and your father, and now that's going to change. You may have to move. You may live in two different homes. You may change schools. You'll probably see each parent less often than you are used to. New people, such as stepparents, half sisters, or half brothers, may come into your life.

Most children feel sad, angry, scared, and confused when their parents divorce. Sometimes they blame themselves for the divorce. It almost always takes a long time for life to feel normal again.

If they are going through a divorce right now, your parents are not happy together. Some divorcing parents fight a lot. Others just stop talking to each other. If any of this is going on in your home, it may be really hard to come home from school and see such unhappy people. It can make you very unhappy. You probably have a lot of worries and a lot of questions about what divorce is and what's going to happen to you.

Divorce is all around us. In the United States, half of all marriages end in divorce. Many divorcing couples have children. Unfortunately, knowing this doesn't make your parents' divorce any easier for you to handle.

This book will go over some of the reasons why couples divorce. It will discuss the legal matters involved in divorce. It will describe how children often feel about their parents' divorce. It will suggest some ways to deal with the problems of divorce.

Reading this book is a good way to begin to understand divorce. If you have questions or concerns about what you read, share them with your friends, parents, or teachers.

When parents spend much of their time together fighting, this may be a sign that they are unhappy in their marriage.

DIVORCE: THE PARENTS

A group of parents are talking together. They have joined a divorce support group, and they are discussing why they have chosen to divorce, and how it feels.

Mr. Van Pelt: I think what happened to us is pretty common. When my wife and I married, I expected our marriage to last forever. I took my wedding vows very seriously: "I promise to love and care for you so long as we both shall live." We married, we bought a house, we put our money together, and we had children. I thought we would live together forever as one happy family. Things didn't work out that way. She just stopped loving me. We could stay together, but neither of us would be happy.

Mr. Rosenberg: My wife just told me that she's involved with another man. She loves him and wants to be with him instead of me. Problems always come up in a marriage. Some of the problems can be solved. Others can't be. Ours can't be. When the problems can't be solved, sometimes divorce is the only answer.

Mrs. Kerr: My husband is at work all the time. He comes home late every night. He leaves for work early the next morning. We never spend any time together anymore. He never spends time with the kids.

Mrs. Davis: My husband is not the man I married. He has changed. He's drunk all the time. He hits me. I've seen him hit the children. No one is safe living in our house with that man. We have to split up—I have to protect myself and the children.

Mr. Lopez: My wife and I just drifted apart. We're no longer interested in the same activities. I feel like I'm living with a stranger. We married when we were very young—still in high school. I guess we grew up later. And when we grew up, we found out that we want

Sometimes partners drift apart. In a way they outgrow each other.

different things from life. Yet we still care about each other. It took a long time to figure this out, but now we're afraid that as long as we stay together, we'll both be unhappy.

WHAT'S THE BEST THING TO DO?

Mr. Rosenberg: We talked about divorce once or twice, but we were always against the idea. We thought it would be bad for the kids. Our children are eight, five, and two years old. Now what will a divorce do to them? It's tearing me apart. I don't know which is worse for the kids: living with two people who fight all the time or seeing their parents break up. Once everything settles down, maybe we'd all be much happier living apart. I don't know. I'm scared for me and for them.

Mr. Lopez: My wife and I dreamed of being together forever. We wanted to try everything before taking the final step—divorce. We tried working things out on our own, but we weren't making any progress. Every discussion ended in a fight. We finally went to a marriage counselor. Even though she helped us a lot, we weren't able to work out our problems.

Mrs. Davis: The only way I could get him out of the house was to suggest a trial separation. I couldn't believe he agreed to it without a huge battle. He moved out of the house and found an apartment on the other side of town. I was very relieved to have him gone. A real trial

Some partners realize that they can no longer live together, and one partner usually moves out.

separation may work for some couples who realize they could never really split up. Then they come back together. But I never intended to take him back. The kids and I—we all knew right away that we were happier with him out of the house.

Mrs. Davis: Even though I knew divorce was for the best, I worried all the time. I worried about everything. I worried about what the divorce would do to me. I worried about whether my husband could make it without me. I worried about the children. I worried about how I was going to support myself and the children. I worried about where I'd live. I worried about where the children would live.

Mr. Van Pelt: I worried that I'd never again have someone to love.

Mrs. Kerr: I worried. I was also angry. I was angry at myself. I was angry at my husband. And I was ashamed. I felt like a failure. The marriage I had worked so hard on was falling apart.

Mrs. Davis: On top of everything else, I was scared.

Mr. Lopez: My wife and I spent a lot of time angry at each other. We blamed each other for the divorce. We argued for months about whose fault it was. We each used to tell the kids that it was the other parent's fault. That was probably the most useless thing we could have done. In the end it doesn't really matter whose fault it is. Arguing about that didn't make the problem go away. It didn't stop the divorce from happening. It only made living with it more difficult—for all of us.

DIVORCE: THE CHILDREN

When parents decide to divorce, it affects everything about their lives. It also affects everything in their children's lives. It raises a lot of questions and changes a lot of plans. A child whose parents choose to divorce will have very strong feelings about their decision.

HEARING THE NEWS

A group of kids are talking together. They have joined a support group, and they are discussing how they heard that their parents were divorcing, and how they reacted.

Meghan: My parents kept it all a big secret. They were thinking and talking about a divorce for two years before they said anything to me. Then one day there was this big "we need to talk" family meeting, and they sprang it on me: "We're getting a divorce." I was shocked.

Jason: My parents didn't say anything for a while, either. But it wasn't much of a secret. I guess they tried to protect me by not saying anything. But I heard them fighting in their room. I saw the looks they gave each other. I could tell when Mom had been crying. At dinner no one talked. Everything was tense. Dad would find excuses to work late. I'd seen my two best friends go through this, so I knew what was coming.

Keisha: My mom was very open about her problems with my dad. She'd been telling me since last year, "I don't know how much longer your daddy's going to be living here, honey. He's found a new girlfriend." It was hard to listen to Mom talk about all this, but at least when the divorce came, it wasn't much of a surprise. I was upset, but it was also a relief in a lot of ways. So I think it was good that Mom talked about it so much.

Jordan: My mom talked about it, too, and I hated it! I felt stuck in the middle all the time. Dad would be away, and I'd ask Mom where he was. She'd say something like, "The jerk is probably with one of his girlfriends." I mean, I don't really need to hear this. I don't know if

You probably have many different feelings about your parents' divorce, including anger.

what she said was true. I just knew that life at home was lonely, miserable, and difficult, and I wanted something to change.

HOW IT FEELS WHEN PARENTS SPLIT UP

Mohammed: I feel like no one cares about me. I first heard about the divorce by accident. I heard Mom tell a friend that she and Dad were thinking about splitting up. What about me? When was she planning to tell me? No one said anything to me about it. I wish they had asked my opinion or at least given me some warning. What they do affects me, too.

Meghan: I think maybe this is all my fault. Maybe if I did more chores around the house my parents would fight less. Maybe if I got better grades they would have fewer problems to deal with. Maybe then they wouldn't want a divorce.

Jordan: I want them to stay together. I wish I knew what to do. I would do anything to keep us all together.

Stefanie: I was shocked. Sure, I knew there were some problems. But the word "divorce" sounded so final to me. It was like a death. I screamed when my parents told me. I told them that they were bad parents. I told them that they didn't love me. I told them that they should have talked to me before making the decision. I spent the next week in my room crying.

ADJUSTING
TO THE
DIVORCE

When you first hear about your parents' divorce, you're likely to have a jumble of feelings. You may be very upset. You may be angry one minute and depressed the next. You may try to pretend that it's not happening. Some young people think that if they ignore the news, it will go away. It's their way of coping with the facts.

None of these reactions is unusual. Very upsetting news—whether it's news of a divorce, a death, a serious injury, or something else that you wish weren't happening—is hard to accept. It takes time to adjust.

Some of these comments might sound like something you've been saying or thinking:

WANTING TO CHANGE THINGS

"Dad and Mom are having problems, but I'm going to make them better. I'm going to behave so well that they will realize we can live together happily."

"Mom, you're making a big mistake. Let me talk to Dad and make him change his mind."

"Tell me what I can do to stop this from happening."

"I can save my parents' marriage."

DENYING THAT ANYTHING'S WRONG

"My parents are doing fine. Dad's away for a while, but he'll come back."

"They say they're going to split up, but they won't. They wouldn't."

"Don't tell me I need to learn to face this. They'll change their minds. Why waste energy wondering what divorce would be like when I know they're not going to split up?"

"This isn't a problem for me. I'm fine. I don't really care if they stay together or not."

BEING ANGRY AND AFRAID

"Why are they doing this to me? What did I do to deserve this?"

"I don't want them to split up. It's going to make my life very difficult, and that's not fair to me."

"How am I going to survive without both of them?"

"Will Mom really come to visit me after she moves out?"

FEELING DEPRESSED

"I'll never see Dad again."

"Life will never be the same."

"It's like someone died. People say I'm supposed to 'get on with my life.' How can I, with this stupid new arrangement?"

"I can't stop crying."

A period of sadness is common when a family breaks up. It will take time to adjust to the changes in your life.

FEELING ABANDONED

"Dad's gone. If he cared about us, he would have stayed. He never loved us. I hate him."

"Mom used to be my best friend. Now that she has a new boyfriend, I'm not important to her anymore."

"When Dad is late picking me up, I become really angry. Mom says I'm being immature and unfair. Dad has the right to have a life, she says. Well, I used to be more a part of his life, and I feel like I'm less a part of it now."

"I can't talk to Mom anymore since the divorce. She's so upset. Compared to her, I feel like my problems are too unimportant to talk about."

ACCEPTING THE NEWS

"It's not so bad. It's kind of fun staying at Dad's house on the weekends."

"Mom's new boyfriend is OK, I guess. Anyway, he's a good cook."

"It's not as good as it was when they were together, for sure, but it's not so awful anymore. I think someday I'll be used to this. I'm not used to it yet, but I think I'll be OK."

DEALING WITH YOUR FEELINGS

Patti was miserable when her parents split up. The day her father moved out, Patti locked herself in her bedroom. She went to school the next day, but at school she refused to talk to anyone. After school she went right back into her room. She did this every day for weeks. She stopped studying. She stopped eating.

Patti's mother invited Patti's favorite aunt, Betsy, to come for a visit. The first couple of days after Betsy arrived, Patti's behavior didn't change. Soon, though, Patti started talking to her aunt. She told Aunt Betsy about how miserable and confused she was. She said that she felt both of her parents had abandoned her.

Aunt Betsy didn't say much. She gave Patti a lot of hugs, and she answered her questions honestly. She told Patti that whether she believed it or not, things would be better in time.

After her aunt left, Patti was still very unhappy, but she felt a little better. She was able to start concentrating on her schoolwork again. She began talking to her

It may help to talk to someone about how upset you are—someone who will understand your feelings and take them seriously.

friends. And in time she even began talking to her mother and her father about the divorce.

WHAT DOESN'T WORK

Patti's way of coping with her parents' divorce was to hide from it. Jamal had a different way, but it wasn't any easier. If you had talked to Jamal then, you wouldn't even have known that his family had gone through a divorce. He appeared happy, he spent time with his friends, and he never said a word about what was going on at home. But inside Jamal was suffering. He had trouble sleeping. He had to work a lot harder than he did before the divorce to concentrate on his school-work. Like Patti, Jamal would have felt better if he had faced his problems.

Some young people work very hard to ignore their feelings. If you're like Jamal, you might think that you're doing all right now. But you may find that the divorce will affect you years later. Holding your feelings in, as Patti and Jamal did, only makes the problems worse. It will also take longer for the problems to go away. The sooner you decide to face all the

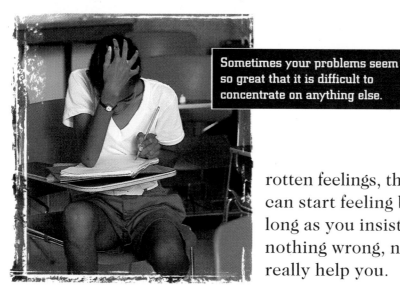

Sometimes your problems seem so great that it is difficult to concentrate on anything else.

rotten feelings, the sooner you can start feeling better. But as long as you insist that there's nothing wrong, no one can really help you.

WHAT DOES WORK

Nothing you do can stop the divorce, but there are things you can do to make yourself feel better. Find a healthy outlet for your feelings. If you're sad, cry. If you're angry, find a way to let out some of that anger. Exercise is a good way. It might take a lot of basketball games to get rid of all your energy, but you'll feel better sooner.

One of the best things you can do for yourself is to talk about your feelings. If you don't want to talk to your parents, talk to your siblings or your friends. They care about you, and they want to help you.

Do you know any other kids whose parents have split up? In some cities there are groups for young people whose parents are divorcing. If you ask at your school or at a local youth center, you may find just such a group. If there isn't one, why not start one? Divorce is so common in America today, you're sure to find other kids with similar problems.

You'll probably find that you have some questions your friends can't answer. When these questions come up, ask your parents if you can talk about them together. Tell them that you need some answers so you can start to accept the new situation. Your parents care about you. They want to make the divorce as easy as possible on you. Ask for help, and they will do whatever they can.

Statistics

Number of married Americans: 115.1 million (61% of adults)
Number of divorced Americans: 17.4 million (9.1% of adults)
Number of single men living with children: 1.3 million (1% of all homes)
Number of single women living with children: 7.6 million (8% of all homes)
Number of marriages each year: 2.3 million
Number of divorces each year: 1.2 million

Percentage of divorces that involve children: over 70
Percentage of divorced people who remarry: 80
Percentage of women who receive alimony after a divorce: 10–15
Percentage of men who are granted sole custody of their children after divorce: 10

Average age of the first marriage for women and for men: 24 and 26
Average age of divorce for women and for men: 33 and 35
Average age of remarriage for women and for men: 34 and 37
Average duration of marriage: 7 years

Source: *Statistical Abstract of the United States, 1995: The National Data Book*
(U.S. Department of Commerce, Bureau of the Census).

SEPARATING COMBINED LIVES

Marriage is the joining of two lives. When adults marry, they make a legal contract to share certain things. Most married couples agree to take care of each other and to be faithful to one another. They promise that they will do everything they can to help each other through troubled times. Most couples agree to live together and to combine their money and their possessions. If they later have children, both parents will be equally responsible for supporting and raising those children.

If two married people decide later that they cannot do what they promised to do, the only way they can legally end their marriage is through a divorce. A divorce is a legal procedure in which the partners divide their combined lives. They split all the property and responsibilities they shared during the marriage. They must find a way to divide everything so that it's fair to everyone involved, including the children.

The divorce between Lionel's parents, Mr. and Mrs. Brown, is typical. Lionel's parents met when they were in college. They married right after graduation. They found an apartment together. They both had jobs, and they agreed that all the money they earned on their jobs would be put into a joint bank account. They made decisions together, such as whether to have children and where and when to buy a house. When they bought their car and their house, they took out loans to pay for them. The couple shared their income and their debts.

As time went by, Mr. and Mrs. Brown became less and less happy together. After ten years of marriage, when Lionel was six years old, the Browns realized that they wanted to divorce.

By that time there was no easy way to tell what belonged to Mr. Brown and what belonged to Mrs. Brown. Everything belonged to the two of them equally. But in order to finalize the divorce, the Browns had to find a way to divide their money, their house, their car, and their debts. And they had to make some hard decisions about Lionel's future.

MONEY AND PROPERTY

Lionel's parents didn't have too much trouble dividing their property. After they separated their clothing and other personal items, they each made a list of things they wanted, such as furniture, books, and housewares. Mrs. Brown took everything on her list that wasn't on Mr. Brown's, and he took everything that she didn't include on her list. Then they negotiated over the things they both wanted. To keep the division fair, they made sure that the value of what Mrs. Brown took was about the same as the value of what Mr. Brown was taking. For example, they agreed that she would keep the car, so he received more of their savings. In order to pay off the loans on the house and the car, they decided to sell the house and each find an apartment to rent.

Moving to a new place is probably the last thing you want to do. Allow yourself some time to adjust to the change.

ALIMONY

In some families only one partner works to earn money. The other stays home to raise the children or take care of the house. If the couple splits up, the partner who stayed at home will be left without an income. Often that partner has no recent job experience, and it may be hard for her or him to find paying work.

To solve this problem, one partner may make regular payments to the other partner. These payments are called alimony. The jobless partner uses the money for housing, food, clothing, and other expenses. If she or he remarries or begins making enough money to become self-supporting, the alimony payments stop.

THE CHILDREN

For Mr. and Mrs. Brown, making decisions about money and cars was much easier than making decisions about their son. They couldn't simply split Lionel down the middle. They both loved Lionel. They both insisted that he remain a part of each of their lives. They knew that Lionel should stay in close contact with both parents, so they agreed to live in the same neighborhood.

Mr. and Mrs. Brown agreed to share custody of Lionel. The first half of the week, they decided, Lionel would live with his dad. The second half of the week, he would stay with his mom. The new routine took some time for everyone to become used to, but after a while, it worked out.

WHERE WILL YOU LIVE?

These are the most common custody arrangements for a family that is divorced:

▶ **Joint custody** In a joint-custody arrangement, a child lives part-time with each parent. Some children of divorced parents spend half a week with one parent and half a week with the other, like Lionel. Others spend a year with one parent and then a year with the other, or spend the school year with one parent and summer vacations with the other.

▶ **Sole custody** For some families it makes the most sense for the children to live full-time with one parent. Today sole custody is less common than joint custody. But it is the best arrangement if the parents live far apart, if one parent has been abusive, or if one parent doesn't feel that he or she can handle the responsibility.

▶ **Split custody** In a split custody arrangement, the children are divided between the parents. One parent takes sole responsibility for some of the children, and the other parent takes responsibility for the others. A common arrangement is for the mother to raise the girls, while the father raises the boys. Another is for one parent to take the older children and the other to take the younger children.

▶ **Third-party custody** In some cases it may be best for a child to live with someone other than his or her parents. For example, maybe both parents have moved to other neighborhoods, but the child doesn't want to change schools. Or maybe the parents don't have the time or the room to care for children. In rare situations like these, the children might live with a grandparent or a family friend.

If you end up living with one parent, the other parent will probably have visitation rights. This means that you'll be able to spend some days, weekends, or vacations with that parent, away from the parent you live with.

WHO WILL MAKE DECISIONS FOR YOU?

Where you will live is only one decision your parents will make. They will also have to agree on some others. Will you change schools? Will you have a religious education? Should you go to college? What if you become ill? Who will decide which doctor you should see? A married couple makes these decisions together. But a divorced couple may need to come to a different arrangement.

Generally if parents share custody, they share major decisions in just this way. The arrangement worked for the Browns because they were able to remain friendly after the divorce. Other parents may need to set up an agreement that doesn't involve seeing each other.

WHO WILL SUPPORT YOU?

No matter who is making decisions about your life, both of your parents remain responsible for supporting you. Both parents must share the costs of raising the child. This includes the costs of food, clothing, medical bills, education, and other needs.

This is true even if the child lives full-time with only one parent. The other parent—the noncustodial parent—must make child support payments to the custodial parent. The money can be used only for the child's needs, not for general family expenses.

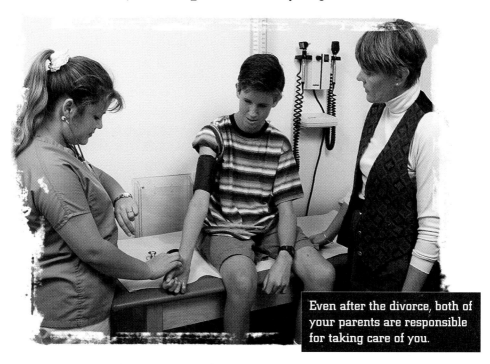

Even after the divorce, both of your parents are responsible for taking care of you.

MAKING TOUGH DECISIONS

Lionel's parents were able to work things out peacefully. They could agree about most of the decisions they needed to make about their property and about how to raise Lionel. Sometimes a divorcing couple can't work things out so easily. Some divorcing couples won't talk to each other. Others simply can't figure out an agreement that seems fair to everyone.

When a couple can't make these decisions on their own, they need to ask someone else for help. They might ask a family member or friend. More often, however, they go to a professional mediator or a family court judge.

MEDIATION

A mediator is a problem solver for people who are trying to come to a fair agreement. Divorce mediators help couples work together to divide property and settle issues in a way that is fair to both partners.

Mediators never take sides. Instead they try to figure out what to do to make everyone feel as satisfied as possible in a difficult situation. Often mediators can come up with compromises that the couple hadn't thought of. Because people who are divorcing are often

A mediator helps people to reach an agreement that is fair to both parties.

upset or angry, they may have trouble seeing the big picture or even thinking about the future. Since a mediator's emotions are not tied up in the divorce, he or she can focus on things that the couple can't.

For example, Mr. and Mrs. Hirashi agreed that their two daughters should live with their mother after the divorce. But one daughter, Viola, needed physical therapy twice a week. Mr. Hirashi had a flexible work schedule, so it had always been his job to drive Viola to the physical therapy center. Their new living arrangement, though, would require Mr. Hirashi to pick up Viola at school, drive 30 miles to the physical therapy center, and then drive her back to Mrs. Hirashi's house, which was 20 miles from his own home. He didn't think it was fair for him to have to do this if he wasn't living with the children. Mrs. Hirashi wasn't able to change her schedule to accommodate Viola's physical therapy. The Hirashis couldn't find a solution.

Finally they talked with a mediator. The mediator asked if it might be worth paying a little more money to have a physical therapist visit Viola at home to do the therapy. This was a solution that neither parent had considered. They agreed that it was worth the extra expense, and they accepted the mediator's suggestion.

FAMILY COURT

It's best for everyone if a couple can agree—alone or with a mediator—on what to do about their children, money, and property. Once they've worked out the details, all they need to do is submit their plan to a family court judge. If the plan appears fair, the judge will grant the divorce. This is called an uncontested divorce. These days most divorces are uncontested.

Sometimes, however, a couple cannot reach an agreement. A divorce in which the partners cannot agree is called a contested divorce. A contested divorce requires a court trial. During the trial, each partner presents his or her side of the disagreement. The judge listens to both sides and comes up with a fair settlement. The judge then decides who receives what property and makes arrangements for the children. Both partners must accept the judge's decision.

WHAT DO YOU WANT?

If your parents are negotiating a divorce, they are making a lot of decisions about you and your future. It's important that you understand that no one will make any final decisions without talking to you. You probably have some opinions about where you want to live and how much time you want to spend with each of your parents. Your opinions and feelings are very important. Your parents, the mediator, and the judge will want to hear from you in order to work out the arrangement that is best for you.

Of course what most children really want is to have their parents change their minds about the divorce. They want to live with both parents all the time. But once the parents agree that that's not going to happen, the task is to decide on a second-best choice.

If you're like most kids, you may find it hard to decide where you want to live. You probably love both your parents equally. You don't want to be forced to take sides, or to choose a favorite. Even if there is one parent you'd rather live with, you may be afraid to say so. You may be afraid of hurting the other parent's feelings. But at the same time, you may not want to split your life between two homes. That's natural. Your parents understand how hard the divorce is on you, and it's best to be honest about how you feel. Things can always be changed later, and no matter what, you'll probably be able to stay in close touch with both of your parents.

A NEW LIFE

Q: How old were you when your parents divorced?

A: I was ten.

Q: How did you feel when you found out about the divorce?

A: At first I was really upset and angry. I screamed a lot. I cried a lot. I wanted to blame somebody, so I blamed my dad. It wasn't really his fault, though. I didn't talk to him much for a few months. I couldn't concentrate on my homework, and I gained a lot of weight. Both my parents were really worried about me. They sent me to a counselor, and I'm doing a lot better now.

Q: How do you feel about your parents' divorce now?

A: It really took two years for things to finally settle down. I'm lucky 'cause I didn't have to change schools. Now I'm used to living in two different houses. I don't feel so angry anymore. I have to admit—my parents seem a lot happier than they were when they were married. I guess it's best in the end, but I still miss the old days.

GROWING USED TO IT

When Karen's parents told her that they were thinking about divorcing, she felt as if her world was ending. She was stunned. She panicked. She couldn't see any future for herself. She wondered if she'd ever see her father again. Although she was only 11 years old, she worried about whether both of her parents would come to her college graduation or her wedding. She was sure that she would never become used to this change in her life.

Karen begged her parents to give their marriage another try. Her parents agreed. They couldn't make up their minds whether divorce would be best. So, because they weren't sure, and for Karen's sake, they decided to stay together.

Things didn't work out the way Karen or her parents had hoped. Her parents stayed married, and she was able to see them both every day, but everyone could tell that no one was happy. Karen's parents continued to have problems. Karen knew that they were fighting and trying to hide their fights from her. She knew that the family couldn't continue like this.

In time the situation grew worse. Because her parents were so unhappy, Karen became depressed. She didn't like to be at home. She never knew when an argument would start. She felt that she couldn't depend on her parents to help her with her own problems.

When Karen turned 13, she admitted to herself that things weren't working. She realized that she might be happier if her parents split up. The three of them talked it over and agreed that a divorce would be best for everyone.

And, like most children, Karen did find a way to live with the divorce. She still hates it, but she knows that it's better than the way things were. She has learned to accept her new life. Now one year after the divorce was final, Karen feels that her life is starting to seem normal again.

It's going to take some time for you to adjust to your new life, too. Divorce causes big changes. After the divorce, you won't see either parent as much as you used to. Since living apart costs more than living together, both parents may have to spend more time at work. They may also spend time making new friends—maybe even dating. As a result, even the parent you live with will have less time to spend with you.

You'll have other adjustments to make, too. You may have to move to a new home. You may have to adjust to traveling between two homes. You may have to transfer to a different school.

Most children of divorced parents say the first two years are the hardest. After that they become accustomed to their new lives and begin to feel happy again.

COMPETITION FOR AFFECTION

Many children of divorced parents find that their parents act oddly after the divorce. Some parents feel lonely. Some seem needy. Others become overly protective of their children. Some parents start to compete with each other for the affection or attention of their children. This can be very difficult and awkward for the children.

Keisha: Whenever I saw my dad, he would say rotten things about my mom: "The divorce was her fault—you know that, don't you, Keisha? I wanted to stay together, but your mother said she had to have her freedom." I hated when he said stuff like that. I found it hard to visit Dad because I knew he was going to say something mean about Mom.

Jason: My parents played some awful games. One would ask me to deliver messages to the other one. I mean, not just messages like, "Tell your father I need to talk to him about your summer plans," but little comments like, "Tell your mother that if she loved you, she'd buy you better shoes." I mean, that message wasn't for Mom. It was for me. I guess it was supposed to make me angry at her or like him better or something.

Mohammed: My parents drive me nuts with all their questions. I'll come back from my week at Dad's house, and Mom will ask, like she's being really casual, "How are your father and his girlfriend doing?" Then, when I go back to Dad's, he's asking, "Did your mother mention if she's dating anyone?" I mean, what am I supposed to do—tattle on my parents?

Meghan: After the divorce, when I stayed with my father, he would let me do anything I wanted. He let me rent movies that my mother would never let me see. He let me stay up as late as I wanted. He even let me eat junk food, something that he never let me do before the divorce. Mom did the same sort of thing. Before the divorce I used to have to help make dinner and do the laundry. Now Mom does it all. It was fun at first, but it felt stupid after a while. I mean, what are they doing—competing to be the "good parent?"

Cecily: What my parents do is each try to make the other one angry—and I usually am stuck in the middle of it. Like, last week, my mother was supposed to pick me up at Dad's house at four. She knew he had a date, and she thought it would be fun to make him miss his date, so she came an hour late. Sure it messed up Dad's date, but it also made me miss soccer practice.

Stefanie: My parents just make me angry. Mom can't even pick me up at Dad's without saying something nasty to him. I wish I were old enough to travel back and forth by myself so that they wouldn't have to see each other.

DEALING WITH DIFFICULT PARENTS

Some couples stay on good terms after the divorce. They think of each other as friends. They enjoy talking to each other when they drop off or pick up their children. They both still care about each other, and each truly wants the other to be happy.

But other divorced people don't find it easy to be friends. They may feel angry, jealous, or lonely. They may become competitive. This is usually very hard on the children.

Some children are afraid to speak up about this. They're aware that their parents are going through difficult times. They know that the divorce was hard on both of them. But if your parents are treating you unfairly, it's up to you to say something. Often parents just don't realize what they are doing. If you tell your parents that what they say or do makes you uncomfortable, they probably will stop.

A HEALTHIER PLACE

At times as you try to adjust to the divorce, you'll probably feel upset. You may wish that your life could be the way it used to be. But keep in mind that your life before the divorce wasn't perfect, either.

Many people tend to remember only the good times when they think about the past. They remember the birthday parties and family vacations. They forget about the anger and the fighting that sometimes made the house an unhappy place. When you think about the past, be sure to think about the bad things as well as the good times. Otherwise you'll have a hard time putting it all behind you.

You can't make the divorce go away. But you can make the best of your new life. It may take some time, but you will learn to appreciate the new calm in your household. Your parents, too, will learn to adjust. After some time they'll feel better about their lives. Life is going to be different from now on. But in some ways it may be better than it was.

REMARRIAGE AND NEW FAMILIES

DATING

A brother and sister talk about what happened when their mother started to date following her divorce.

March

James: Mom's got a date!?

Lili: Yeah. So what's so strange about that?

James: You don't think it's strange—or weird—to think of Mom holding hands with some guy? Or kissing some guy? Some stranger? Ick! Is she going to have him over for dinner and stuff?

Lili: Probably. I mean, she's known him for a few months. She says he's really nice. And she says he's asked her if he could take us on a camping trip.

James: I don't want to go.

Lili: James, I know this is weird for you. It's weird for me. But, you know, it's good for Mom. She and Dad have been divorced for nearly a year. What's she supposed to do? She needs friends, just like you and I do. Do you want her to be lonely for the rest of her life?

Sooner or later your parents will probably want to meet new people, and they may fall in love again.

May

James: I think Mom's in love.

Lili: What makes you think so?

James: She seems so happy all the time. And she's nicer than she's ever been since the divorce. I haven't seen her cry in a long time. And she's stopped asking me questions about Dad. Have you noticed, if I say anything nice about Stuart, her whole face lights up?

Lili: I guess she remembers how you felt about Stuart when you first met him.

James: Yeah. I guess he's good for her, though. I'm glad she's happy.

Lili: And don't you like Stuart? I do. He's fun to be with. I hope he and Mom stay together.

September

James: What happened with Mom and Stuart?

Lili: Mom said it didn't work out. It was fun for a while, she said, but Stuart isn't someone she wants to stay with forever.

James: I'm going to miss him.

Lili: Yeah, me too. I feel bad for Mom and for us.

It can be strange to think of your parents going out on dates. It's even stranger to imagine them falling in love with other people. But there's a good side to this. When people fall in love, they become happier. And when people are happier, they're more fun to be with.

A lot of young people don't like their parents' new friends at first. But usually, if you give the new friend a chance, you'll find something special about him or her. After all, if your parent likes the person, there must be some things for you to like about him or her.

Sometimes, however, a parent's new relationship doesn't work out, and the children are very disappointed. For this reason it's best not to focus too much on your parents' social life. Enjoy the people your parents introduce you to, but give them some time and some privacy to develop their own relationships. After all, that's probably how you would like them to treat you when you start dating.

NEW FAMILY MEMBERS

Going through a divorce is a temporary process. In time the negotiations between your parents will end. All the issues of who will live where and how often you will see your parents will be settled. Routines will be established. Then you have the rest of your life to look forward to. It will be different from the life you used to have. It will have good differences and bad differences. You can probably list some of the bad differences:

- You won't see both of your parents as often as you used to.
- Your parents may be sad, lonely, or angry at times.
- There may be some financial difficulties.
- You may have to adjust to a new living arrangement.

So what are the good differences? There will probably be less tension and fighting in your home. Your life may be more peaceful. The divorce gives each of your parents a chance to work out a better life and maybe to find a new partner. Many divorced parents remarry. A parent's remarriage will probably seem strange to you at first, but it may turn out to be wonderful.

HOW PARENTS FEEL ABOUT DATING AGAIN

Mr. Van Pelt: I was miserable after the divorce. I thought no one would ever love me again. I felt bad for myself. I felt bad for the kids. Friends would try to introduce me to women, but I thought it would be a waste of time. When I met Michelle, I was probably not very nice to her at first. But she understood what I was going through and let me take things slowly. We dated for a year before I let myself admit that I really liked having her in my life.

Mrs. Kerr: Six months after the divorce, I started dating. What was most important to me was that the men I dated wanted to be part of a family. It wasn't enough that they wanted to be with me. A few of my first dates were family dinners. It probably was hard on the men, but if they didn't enjoy a noisy, busy, chaotic evening, they weren't going to be happy with me and the four children.

Mrs. Davis: What made me know that Sammy was right for me was the feelings he and my daughter Lucy had for each other. One day Lucy had some crisis that couldn't wait, and she couldn't find me. She went to visit Sammy at his store. She told him she had a problem, and he immediately stopped what he was doing. He took her out for a soda, and they talked. It was wonderful. What Lucy did showed me that she felt she could count on Sammy for advice. What Sammy did showed me that Lucy was right.

Mr. Lopez: The whole time I was dating Ellie, I was very honest with my kids. I even asked if they would let me ask her to marry me. After the wedding I frequently checked with them to see if they had any bad feelings about having a second mom. I wanted to make sure they didn't think that Ellie was trying to replace their real mother. Ellie had two young daughters, too, and I wanted to make sure they felt OK about having new little sisters.

The remarriage of a parent may bring unexpected rewards—and a new friend—into your life.

HOW CHILDREN FEEL ABOUT THEIR PARENTS' DATING

Cecily: When Dad started dating Sarah, it was weird. He and I had less time to spend alone together. Whenever I wanted to do something with Dad, he'd say, "Can I bring Sarah along?" What could I say? I was happy for him, but I missed our father-daughter times.

Meghan: I hated Mom's new husband at first. He changed everything at home. He was a stranger, yet suddenly he was telling me what I could and couldn't do. Mom was so in love with him that she never had time for me. But he wasn't going to go away. So I figured, I can either mope about it forever, or I can try to find something to like about him. It's not easy. He's not my father, and I hate that I see him every day, and I see Dad only twice a year.

Keisha: The best part was that Dad's new wife has two daughters. All at once I had sisters! I always wanted a sister.

Mohammed: For ten years I was an only child. Then, when Mom remarried, I found myself with a brother. Having him move into my house was strange. I had to share things. But I quickly got used to having him around. Now that we've been together for a year, I like it. I have someone I can really talk to. It's great, because my stepbrother is a year older than me, and his parents split up two years before mine did. So he knows what I've been going through. He's helped me a lot.

A NEW FAMILY

If your parents remarry, it will take time and patience to make your new family work. You'll have to try hard to be fair to these new family members. But if you make an honest effort, things will probably come together. After some time, you'll all feel comfortable, like a family.

Of course things will never be perfect. Like any family, you'll probably have fights and disagreements. But like any family, you'll probably develop strong bonds that will last a lifetime.

As years go by, you'll discover that you're very lucky. You'll have a caring family—maybe even two caring families. You'll have new people in your life whom you may grow to love. You'll have parents who are happier than they were when they were together. In the end you may even feel that your parents' divorce was the best thing that could have happened.

alimony: Money paid to a separated or divorced spouse for the support of that spouse.

child support: Money paid to the divorced parent who has custody of the child, to be used for the care of that child.

contested divorce: A divorce in which both partners cannot agree on the division of their joint property and the care of their children.

contract: A legally binding agreement between people.

custodial parent: The parent who has the primary responsibility for the care of the child; the parent with whom the child lives.

custody: The legal responsibility to care for, as for a child.

divorce: The legal ending of a marriage.

mediation: Help in settling a dispute, provided by someone who is not directly involved.

negotiate: To talk over and arrange terms, as in a disagreement.

trial separation: When a married couple stays married, but partners choose to live separately for a period of time.

uncontested divorce: A divorce in which both partners agree about the division of their joint property and the care of their children.

visitation: Time spent by a child with the noncustodial parent.

WHERE TO GO FOR HELP

If you need someone to talk to about what's going on, tell your parents or a school counselor. Many young people find that what they really need is to talk with others who are going through or have gone through the same thing they are experiencing. You may find support groups for children of divorced parents at your local community center.

You also may want to contact the local office of Parents Without Partners. This group can be a good resource for your parents as they go through the divorce and afterward, as they go about beginning their new lives. Also, many Parents Without Partners groups have a support group for children of parents who are divorcing or divorced.

HOT LINES

United States

The Nineline
1-800-999-9999

Youth Crisis Hotline
1-800-448-4663

National Runaway
Switchboard
1-800-621-4000

Community Information
and Referral Services
1-800-352-3792

Canada

Families in Transition
2 Carlton Street
Toronto, ON M5B 1J3
1-416-585-9151

Kids Help Phone
2 Bloor Street W.
P.O. Box 513
Toronto, ON M4W 3E2
1-800-668-6868

International

Australian Institute of Family
Studies
300 Queen Street
Melbourne, Victoria 3000

Boeckman, Charles. *Surviving Your Parents' Divorce.* Franklin Watts, 1980.

Bolick, Nancy O. *How to Survive Your Parents' Divorce.* Franklin Watts, 1994.

Booher, Dianna Daniels. *Coping When Your Family Falls Apart.* Julian Messner, 1979.

Brogan, John P., and Ula Maiden. *The Kids' Guide to Divorce.* Ballantine, 1986.

Friedrich, Liz. *Divorce.* Aladdin, 1988.

Goldentyer, Debra. *Parental Divorce.* Raintree Steck-Vaughn, 1995.

Hyde, Margaret O. *My Friend Has Four Parents.* McGraw-Hill, 1981.

LeShan, Eda. *What's Going to Happen to Me?* Four Winds Press, 1978.

Levine, Beth. *Divorce: Young People Caught in the Middle.* Enslow, 1995.

Rofes, Eric E., ed. *The Kids' Book of Divorce: By, for and About Kids.* Random House, 1982.

INDEX